ROSE'S ~~ARE~~ RED, VIOLET'S ~~ARE~~ BLUE

and Other Silly Poems

For my superb nieces, Shenaugh, Heather,
Heidi, and Sarah

How could an uncle get so lucky?

Also by Wallace Tripp:

Granfa' Grig Had a Pig
A Great Big Ugly Man Came Up and Tied His Horse to Me

Compilation and illustrations copyright © 1999 by Wallace Tripp

First Edition

Acknowledgment is given as follows for permission to reprint copyrighted material:

"Palmstroem" from *The Gallows Songs,* by Christian Morgenstern. Copyright © 1963 by Max E. Knight. Reprinted by permission of the University of California Press.

"The Lesser Lynx" from *The Flattered Flying Fish,* by E. V. Rieu. Copyright © 1962 by E. V. Rieu. Reprinted by permission of Richard Rieu.

"I Am Rose" from *The World Is Round,* by Gertrude Stein. Copyright © 1966 by Gertrude Stein. Reprinted by permission of Addison-Wesley Publishing Co., Inc.

Library of Congress Cataloging-in-Publication Data

Rose's are red, Violet's are blue : and other silly poems / compiled and illustrated by
    Wallace Tripp. — 1st ed.
      p.   cm.
    Summary: A collection of silly and amusing poems by American and English writers.
    ISBN 0-316-85440-9
    1. Children's poetry, American. 2. Children's poetry, English. [1. Nonsense verses.
    2. American poetry — Collections. 3. English poetry — Collections.] I. Tripp, Wallace.
    PS586.3.R67 1998
    811.008'09282 — dc21   97-49343

The text for this book was set in Clearface, and the display type is Spumoni.

10 9 8 7 6 5 4 3 2 1

SC

Printed in Hong Kong

ROSE'S ARE RED, VIOLET'S ARE BLUE

and Other Silly Poems

Compiled and Illustrated by

WALLACE TRIPP

Little, Brown and Company

Boston   New York   London

E. V. Rieu

The Lesser Lynx

The laughter of the Lesser Lynx
 Is often insincere;
It pays to be polite, he thinks,
If Royalty is near.

So when the Lion steals his food
Or kicks him from behind,
He smiles, of course—but oh, the rude
Remarks that cross his mind!

Edward Lear

There Was an Old Person of Ware

There was an old person of Ware,
  Who rode on the back of a bear.
When they asked, "Does it trot?" he said, "Certainly not!
He's a Moppsikon Floppsikon bear!"

Moppsikon Floppsikon
motorized bicycle

John Lyly

Cupid and Campaspe

Cupid and my Campaspe played
At cards for kisses; Cupid paid.
He stakes his quiver, bow and arrows,
His mother's doves and team of sparrows;

Loses them too; then down he throws
The coral of his lip, the rose
Growing on's cheek (but none knows how);
With these the crystal of his brow,
And then the dimple of his chin;
All these did my Campaspe win.

At last he bet her both his eyes;
She won, and Cupid blind did rise.
O Love, has she done this to thee?
What shall, alas! become of me?

Artemus Ward

Uncle Simon and Uncle Jim

Uncle Simon he
Clum up a tree
To see what he could see
When presentlee
Uncle Jim
Clum up beside of him
And squatted down by he.

F. C. Burnand

Oh, My Geraldine

Oh, my Geraldine,
No flow'r was ever seen so toodle um.
You are my lum ti toodle lay,
Pretty, pretty queen,
Is rum ti Geraldine and something teen,
More sweet than tiddle lum in May.
Like the star so bright

That somethings all the night,
My Geraldine!
You're fair as the rum ti lim ti sheen,
Hark! there is what—ho!
From something—um, you know,
Dear, what I mean.
Oh! rum! tum!! tum!! my Geraldine.

Oliver Herford

Some Geese

E v-er-y child who has the use
Of his sen-ses knows a goose.
See them un-der-neath the tree
Gath-er round the goose-girl's knee,
While she reads them by the hour
From the works of Scho-pen-hau-er.

How pa-tient-ly the geese at-tend!
But do they re-al-ly com-pre-hend
What Scho-pen-hau-er's driv-ing at?
No, not at all, but what of that?
Nei-ther do I; nei-ther does she;
And, for that mat-ter, nor does he.

Wallace Tripp

Rose's Are Red

R ose's are red,
Violet's are blue;

Similar spots
Are appearing on you.

Lewis Carroll

Jabberwocky

'Twas brillig, and the slithy toves
Did gyre and gimble in the wabe:
All mimsy were the borogoves,
And the mome raths outgrabe.

"Beware the Jabberwock, my son!
The jaws that bite, the claws that catch!
Beware the Jubjub bird, and shun
The frumious Bandersnatch!"

He took his vorpal sword in hand:
Long time the manxome foe he sought—
So rested he by the Tumtum tree,
And stood awhile in thought.

And, as in uffish thought he stood,
The Jabberwock, with eyes of flame,
Came whiffling through the tulgey wood,
And burbled as it came!

One, two! One, two! And through and through
The vorpal blade went snicker-snack!
He left it dead, and with its head
He went galumphing back.

"And hast thou slain the Jabberwock?
Come to my arms, my beamish boy!
O frabjous day! Callooh! Callay!"
He chortled in his joy.

'Twas brillig, and the slithy toves
Did gyre and gimble in the wabe:
All mimsy were the borogoves,
And the mome raths outgrabe.

Gertrude Stein

I Am Rose

I am Rose my eyes are blue
I am Rose and who are you

I am Rose and when I sing
I am Rose like anything

Christian Morgenstern

Palmstroem

Palmstroem stands beside a pond
  where a scarlet handkerchief he wide unfolds;
printed on it is an oak tree and, beyond,
a lone person and a book he holds.

Palmstroem does not dare to blow his nose;
he is plainly one of those
who at times, with sudden start,
feel a reverence for art.

He refolds with tender skill
what he just had spread out clean,
and no gentle soul will wish him ill
if, with nose unblown, he leave the scene.

Henry Wadsworth Longfellow

Excelsior

The shades of night were falling fast,
As through an Alpine village passed
A youth, who bore, 'mid snow and ice,
A banner with the strange device,
Excelsior!

In happy homes he saw the light
Of household fires gleam warm and bright;
Above, the spectral glaciers shone,
And from his lips escaped a groan,
Excelsior!

"Try not the pass!" the old man said;
"Dark lowers the tempest overhead,
The roaring torrent is deep and wide!"
And loud that clarion voice replied,
Excelsior!

"O stay," the maiden said, "and rest
Thy weary head upon this breast!"
A tear stood in his bright blue eye,
But still he answered, with a sigh,
Excelsior!

"Beware the pine-tree's withered branch!
Beware the awful avalanche!"
This was the peasant's last Good-night;
A voice replied, far up the height,
Excelsior!

spelled X-L-C-R

At break of day, as heavenward
The pious monks of Saint Bernard
Uttered the oft-repeated prayer,
A voice cried through the startled air,
Excelsior!

A traveller, by the faithful hound,
Half-buried in the snow was found,
Still grasping in his hands of ice
That banner with the strange device,
Excelsior!

There in the twilight cold and grey,
Lifeless, but beautiful, he lay,
And from the sky, serene and far,
A voice fell, like a falling star,
Excelsior!

Edward Lear

Seven Germans

Seven Germans through my garden lately strayed,
And all on instruments of torture played;
They blew, they screamed, they yelled:
How can I paint
Unless my room is quiet, which it ain't?

A Note about "Jabberwocky"

"Jabberwocky," which is found in *Through the Looking Glass,* is by general acclaim the greatest nonsense poem in the English language. Lewis Carroll's words may seem pure silliness, but elsewhere he supplies clues about the approximate meanings of most of the words:

Brillig means late afternoon.

Slithy is slimy and lithe.

Tove is defined both as a cheese-eating badger with white hair and long back legs and as a badger-lizard-corkscrew combination with stag horns.

To *gyre* means to scratch like a dog or to go round and round like a gyroscope.

To *gimble* is to make holes.

A *wabe* is a grassy hillside.

Mimsy means miserable.

The *borogoves* are shabby parrots with upside-down beaks and no wings.

Mome raths are either homesick green pigs or land turtles.

To *outgrabe* is to issue a bellowing, whistling, sneezing squeak.

Frumious is fuming-furious.

Manxome perhaps means island-dwelling.